Author of the children's book

The Bully in Your Brain

Talk About It! TRAUMA

Healing the Trauma Your Past Left Behind

TERESA G. LUSK

Talk About It!

Healing the Trauma Your Past Left Behind

True Story Publisher in Collaboration with 320 Publishing

ISBN: 979-8-234-11161-6

Cover Design: True Story Publisher

Interior Design: 320 Publishing

Editing: Tammy Warren, 320 Publishing

Printed in the United States of America

U.S. Printing History

First Edition: 2026

TABLE OF CONTENTS

Note From the Author

As a mental health professional, I see patients that have been in therapy for 10 or more years and have not healed. I see doctors prescribe medication instead of fixing root causes. And I see people that use a mental health label to define their lives.

It's not that difficult. You can be healed. You can move forward with your life. I hope this book provides the keys to bring you clarity and peace. Know that you are not permanently damaged.

Teresa G. Lusk

Dedication

This work is dedicated to the people who walked with me, believed in me, and helped bring it to life in more ways than words can fully capture.

To my son, Aslan, thank you for your encouragement, prayers, your imagination, and for dreaming alongside me in these creative endeavors. Your support in moments when the well felt empty meant more than you know. You remind me to keep going, even when strength feels low.

To my dear friend Liz, thank you for walking with me—quite literally at times—and for witnessing the unfolding of big dreams. Your encouragement, presence, and steady belief in what is possible helped give me the courage to step beyond comfort and into new ground.

Tammy, you have been such a blessing in so many ways. From the connections you have provided to now being part of this project, your impact has been meaningful at every step. You will never know the fullness of what your kindness toward me has meant.

To my friend Shelly W. and 320 Publishing, thank you for journeying alongside me through the development of this project. Your generosity in offering your expertise and partnering with me made it possible to shape this work with excellence, clarity, and care. I am also thankful for your team for helping with this project's publishing needs. Every detail matters, every detail counts. Without you, this work would still be sitting in a file. You are highly appreciated.

To all my family and loved ones who have stood with me, supported me, and linked arms in various seasons—your presence has been a gift. You know who you are, and I am deeply grateful.

You all rock in ways that have shaped this journey more than you realize.

About the Author

Teresa G. Lusk is a counselor, executive coach, and communication trainer who has worked with hundreds of individuals in clinical, personal, and professional settings. Her work focuses on emotional healing, trauma recovery, identity, and communication development across personal and professional spaces.

She equips individuals in communication, media, and leadership, helping them strengthen clarity, voice, and personal impact.

BOOKS & PROJECTS:

Teresa is the author of The Bully in Your Brain, a children's book releasing in the same time frame as this work. Additional books and resources can be found at: **truestorypublisher.com**

SPEAKING:

For speaking engagements, visit: **teresalusk.com**

Trauma Defined

Before we begin, it's important to understand how trauma works. Keep this in mind as you read, reflect, and engage in the exercises ahead.

Trauma can be defined in two parts

Interpretation – how the recipient of the event interprets a particular occurrence

Impact – the psychological effects the event has had on that person

This definition will serve as a foundational lens for the concepts, exercises, and insights shared throughout this book. Understanding this allows you to approach your healing with clarity and perspective.

Now, let's talk about the trauma that your past left behind.

Section 1

THE FOUNDATION

Setting the Stage for Healing and Understanding

1

HEALING IS POSSIBLE

So, Let's Identify What's in the Way

I am in what I call a "vocation of hope." When I get the privilege of serving a client, they soon discover that I abound in optimism for healing for all, even beyond the most difficult diagnosis. Whether the medical opinions were given recently or years ago, I will stand in faith for restoration. And the best part is that I don't believe it has to take forever—it can be quick. To deny that the journey toward wholeness hasn't been lengthy for some would be delusional on my part, but my stance is that my job is to lock arms and expect the best outcome, no exceptions.

When I say that my heart burns with hope for individuals, it's nearly searing. While this is not a faith-based book, I do have to give credit to my walk with God, as that is the foundation of all I do and all that has transpired. My faith walk has been my driving force to see people well, healed, and witness them being made whole. And it continues to shape how I approach every person I serve.

Much of what I have helped heal have I had to overcome myself. I believe in raw, real exposure of the feelings and thoughts that are hidden in the deep places that human beings tuck into for survival. My own life experiences speak from firsthand encounters, and they have shaped both my compassion and conviction.

Tell me, how often have you been told that the mental torment called illness is your life's sentence, and to expect to cope, but not fully heal? Are there groups you are part of that share the same sentiments? Do you allow the influence of others who profess that they will never be well—who have adopted a faith in their illness as unchangeable—to shape your destiny? I caution you not to accept others' beliefs about the permanence of illness as your own.

Research has shown that what often aids people in healing faster is determination, positivity, and hope. Recovery is not solely dependent on medication but also on the belief systems and expectations people hold. Hopeful thinking and believing build resilience and optimism.

I wholeheartedly believe the best outcome is possible, especially with the years of testimonies I could share. So what are expectations and optimism for those who have been told that torment is their life sentence to bear? Hope—real, grounded, and unshakable hope.

The Authority Behind My Work

I don't pretend to be qualified beyond my education and my many years of experience. Although I cherish them both, without my experience, I would only be offering knowledge. And, with only an education, it would only be an opinion. I have been working with individuals since 2009 in various capacities and platforms that empower people to heal, and I cannot give credit solely to one of the pieces of my background. All of the opportunities I have engaged in have shaped me into the person that I have grown into. Yet, as an ethical professional, I cannot guarantee healing to anyone. I can, however, confirm that as a therapist, coach, pastoral counselor, faith leader, trainer, and guidance facilitator, I have witnessed repeated, accelerated healing in my meetings. In only one consultation, I have witnessed the unfolding of what many spend months and years navigating.

Not Just Pages in Our Hands

It's imperative that we establish that you are not just reading a book. You are about to engage in words that you may have been waiting for years to hear. If that is not you, no problem, but it still holds much value. For many of you, there are secrets in your hearts that have been waiting to find clarity, validation, understanding, and a sense of wholeness. I trust this is what you will find throughout these pages.

Formed in Real Life, Not Theory

Every person has an amazing whole version of themselves within, and most of the time, it's not that far from their reach. That persona is usually revealed in the peeling back of catastrophic or grievous stories, their impact, and the accepted beliefs they have produced as truth.

Trauma, Trauma Everywhere

The reality is that` there is no shortage of materials on trauma and how to attain restoration. But this book was written with a couple of things in mind that I trust sets it apart from others.

One, I wanted to produce a lighthearted and easily approachable book for a heavy topic. Not all healing has to feel dreadful. In fact, a light and warmhearted experience can assist positively and disarm the part of the brain that resists visiting old memories. Experiencing short bursts of pleasurable encounters rewires the brain into believing that this particular type of experience is not only pleasurable, but beneficial, and eventually, you may even crave it more.

Two, I refused to bombard you with scientific explanations. If that is what you are searching for, I encourage you to read this book in its entirety. Once you complete it in the order it is to be followed, you can decide if you would like a more scientific approach, and continue in your search. I encourage you to be mindful that this experience is not complete unless the exercises have been fully engaged in and completed.

You Were Told Healing Is Weakness

In my beautiful Latino culture, mental health and emotional healing have not been regarded highly. Unfortunately, this is common in many other people groups as well. As a professional and leader who focuses on the "why" behind human behavior, I understand this pattern in many families. This is often because when people are merely trying to survive, emotional needs are not the priority. At times, it is the very hardships they are living in that shape their frame of mind. Eating, paying rent, covering bills, and keeping the children safe and well are higher on the list of needs.

Historically, many people have worked long, demanding hours across generations, leaving little room for emotional vulnerability or reflection. Over time, this way of living has shaped cultures and family patterns, often without anyone realizing when or how it happened.

Healing the Trauma Your Prior Generations Left Behind

Maybe you are having to heal the effects of your own generational instability, a close family member's dysfunction, another's choices, or even uncontrollable circumstances. I acknowledge that some things don't feel fair, such as the pain they caused leaving you with the wreckage. I speak to those who are having to repair the ruins that others passed on to you while you still require emotional and mental support. The hard but honest truth is that almost every single one of us is healing the pain of someone else's past—be it your grandmother, father, mother, etc.

No one escapes this, but the brave decide that to be weak is to leave things unchanged—and they take this on for themselves, for those who will inherit what we leave behind, and for the brokenness of the past. Even those who came before us, formed in deep trauma, can be healed through the decisions *we* make today.

Now, the healthiest approach is to identify, accept, and take steps to rewrite the experience, rewire the brain, and heal heartaches.

The Generational Shift from Emotional Silence to Emotional Visibility

Today, it is evident that our younger generations are reversing this, and it has pushed a movement to normalize emotional health and sharing feelings. Now that this is occurring, we can begin to integrate better pattern building and habits. As with anything, however, everything has an extreme. I would also suggest that we have become too fragile in life, to the point that universities now have "safe spaces" because people cannot handle words and emotions. I have been saying, "More than one thing can be true at the same time." We can do both in a balanced way. Appropriating the correct interpretation and method for each individual circumstance is wisdom. We can be more emotionally aware and not allow our inner condition to define the world around us.

As we have swung quite far to the other side, a popular, stigmatizing trend has taken off. That is, normal human emotional tensions have been labeled with some type of diagnosis. Individuals with everyday problems and common pains have been classified by social media mental health "influencers," and our society is buying it and eating it up. The concern is that once something or someone is labeled, it's difficult to say they or their issue is curable—leaving no room for hope. The good news is that mindsets are adjustable—all day, every day—over any idea or belief system.

You've Seen It One Way—Now Try Another

Maybe you have made up your mind about the avenues to healing you subscribe to, and are now resistant to other restorative modalities. It is true that too much knowledge can inflate your compartment for acquiring new ideas and solutions, even proven ones.

If this is you, and you have spent a generous amount of time researching, TikTok-ing, reading other books, or watching videos, I implore you to set aside what you have known and believed for a short moment. Release those habits that look for errors. And instead look for where my techniques, although elegantly simple, are effective.

Whether you are more clinical or more spiritual, I can assure you that I have utilized this work in both settings and have seen the same level of results, regardless of the domain.

The Fear Behind Talking About It

I want you, my reader, to prepare to cash in on the investment you have made. I would be displeased to think you were not fully equipped to get the most out of any effort you put forth. Remember that talking about the trauma your past left behind is the hard part, and therefore, this book exists. Because of that, I have created an opportunity for you and others searching for ideas for healing to explore some of the options throughout these pages.

Talking about your trauma means that you will write about your experiences, speak about them out loud in a private space, and even record your conversations should you choose to do so. It is necessary to process the words tied to your formative circumstances aloud and in writing since these exercises are being completed through a book, and not in person.

You will come across a more detailed section for this activity, so make a mental note that the writing exercise portion of the book is the bulk of the techniques to attain what you may be searching for.

2

TOOLS, TERMS, AND HOW TO USE THIS BOOK

In the following chapters, you will encounter a plethora of tools including some of my signature vocabulary which will enable you to understand concepts in a deeper, more visual, and impactful way. These are words and phrases that will follow my work for the rest of my career, and will be utilized to train those in the healing industry as well.

In the same manner, the metaphors and methods also carry an impact and function in each one of them. Every single principle and tool has a meaning and intent that has been tried and proven to aid in the journey most of the help seekers have come across.

Tools in Your Toolkit

After I decided I was going back to school to get my master's degree in counseling, I visited a few colleges. It was during one of those meetings that I met a gentleman who was in charge of recruitment for one particular school. That day, my friend Liz happened to accompany me. This man said all the right things. He explained the benefits of their overpriced program – and I mean by the many, many thousands. He shared every bell and whistle the school had to offer and provided their high-quality brochure to take home, but the one memorable thing he kept saying was, "You can put that in your toolkit." It became such a staple statement for Liz and me, and we would say that jokingly to each other over any little silly thing. Months later, Liz gave me a gift bag and asked me to open it. There it was, a canvas pencil pouch with big, black, bold letters. It read, "TOOL KIT."

These are special and comical stories that we will never forget, but have also followed us through the years. Now as I write this book, I am about to pass on to you some tools for your tool kit. I use these instruments daily, such as terms, metaphors, frameworks, and experiences in each of my sessions because they help hundreds of people create a visual of what is going on at a particular time. They assist in understanding life and redefining what has been mislabeled and kept in the dark. The more you understand what is going on at any particular moment, the more healing you are likely to encounter for good.

Mental Metaphors & Methods

Mental metaphors make abstract concepts concrete, creating a pathway for insight, coping, and healing. They help you see patterns in your mind and emotions, such as with "The Bully in Your Brain" or "Disarming Trauma." We will explore these in more detail in a moment.The alternative approaches are the actual methods. Both frameworks are pathways to restoration.

As you explore varying stages of life and challenging journeys, you will be able to apply the various metaphors and methods laid out. You may find that you favor one metaphor or method over another, or find that they all have a perfect place for your processing.

The Bully in Your Brain

Let me describe to you what I call "The Bully in Your Brain," a mental metaphor. Picture with me a symbolic construct that appears as a shadowy tornado with a grumpy face that sits right before your brain to threaten, shout out thoughts, produce distorted imagery, and limit what comes in and what goes out.

This thing stands around—it doesn't sit—it is waiting to tell you a few mean things, even several times a day. This metaphor may be a bit childlike; in fact, it was playful enough that I wrote a children's book titled The Bully in Your Brain to help young ones understand its power and purpose.

This Bully tells you why you are wrong, how ashamed you should feel about the traumatic situation, and how it's all your fault for not speaking up when you "shoulda, coulda, woulda." He reminds you of your age and insists you were old enough when any particular traumatic event happened; therefore, you must be responsible for the circumstances. He produces a mental snapshot followed by internal audio. He says things such as: "I should have tried harder. I could have screamed. I didn't have to tell anyone. I am just weak. I am a crybaby. Others have gone through worse, so why am I crying about something so small?"—and many other mental intrusions throughout the passing days, months, and even years.

The Bully never takes a break, is never on vacation, doesn't shut up, is never wrong in his own mind, and his narrative never really changes. But the one thing that can make him disappear is simpler than you could ever imagine: *telling yourself the truth.*

Designating an image and a name to these intrusions is a tool you can add to your toolkit to help disarm them at any time.

So when you find yourself hemmed in by judgment and intimidation, pull out the image and remember he is only an imagination extinguishable by the facts.

Disarming the Trauma

"Disarming the Trauma" is a signature term I've created. It means facing a memory and releasing the lies, judgments, and feelings it holds—those that keep you trapped in the power of that event in your mind.

For many, once they are exposed to the term, it builds up a "heck-yeah" effect, as it feels like a hostage rescue mission. After all, that is what is occurring. Unvisited, untalked-about trauma can be likened to a non-executed, life-saving operation. I realize it sounds dramatic, but the truth is that when we leave trauma untouched, it handicaps our lives, including our mindsets and what we are willing to pursue and aspire to be. Some have become victims of apathy, stagnation, and a lack of progress in life because the trauma sits in their mind, brain, and body, fully armed.

This is not life's best portion for you. Allowing yourself or someone with great empathy to visit those places with you is the hostage rescue mission in action—the disarming of the trauma that may have been calling for help for many years.

When Grief Comes to Pass

Grief is the profound emotional and total soul reaction to the loss of something, not just someone. The grief portion of this chapter could have been a book all by itself, but for the sake of this discussion, let's address a very condensed version. When an individual has experienced the loss of a person, a job, a spouse, a lifestyle, or something meaningful, the deep soul-mourning responses will make themselves known.

When trauma remains unresolved, grief can take the form of what I call dormant-active grief. It lies in the shadows, quietly influencing thoughts, emotions, and behaviors, often causing unexplained or unrecognized symptoms. Dormant-active grief is the kind that sufferers may not even realize is affecting them, yet it remains present and active.

What this often looks like goes beyond tears—it can include anger, agitation, frustration, irritability, difficulty concentrating, loss of passion for life's activities, fatigue, sleep disturbances, changes in appetite, social withdrawal, guilt, anxiety, restlessness, or a deep sense of emptiness.

There are also those who are aware of what they are experiencing and why, but become overwhelmed by the anxiety it produces. I am going to share something that is not easy to receive, but helpful to hear: *you must allow grief to do its thing as it comes to pass*. Trying to resist it will be one of the most ineffective habits, as grief is a lingering force of its own. It is not like anger, where you can count to ten and interrupt the intensity of its nature. Grief demands to be passed through, and the best thing you can do is embrace its movement along your heart's path.

Of course you can take a walk, think about something positive, pray, etc., but this will simply remove the edge. Once we accept that grief has a season—and that it does get better—we will stop fighting the inevitable and begin to heal.

Through years of working with people, I have found that a large percentage carry unrealized grief, yet it is often the last thing that crosses their minds because grief feels too weighty. It is often reserved for death, but rarely for the forfeiture of opportunities, hopes, dreams, or other meaningful parts of life.

Grief can be present due to the many different losses, gaps, or absences you have experienced in life. Maybe no one ever shared with you that the pain from an attack as a child can result in the loss of innocence. It can arise from a divorce, a missed career opportunity due to a health issue, a poor choice, or any other setback or deprivation. What you refuse to grieve, you will continue to carry.

Triggers: Powerful Signals Leading You to Healing

I invite you to redefine triggers. While we've often been taught to see them as reasons to "lose your mind," triggers can actually be powerful signals of unhealed patterns, experiences, and beliefs that can lead you into healing.

Think of them like a fire alarm that goes off even when there's no real fire—maybe the heat from cooking got a little too high. It means you got close to something that could lose control and become a danger. Triggers work the same way: they alert you when emotions are heating up and something inside needs attention.

Today, we talk about triggers as if we need protection from them instead of addressing what has been left unattended. When you notice your triggers going off, ask yourself: What about this situation set me off? Does it remind me of something from years past that I couldn't control? Does this person resemble someone who caused me harm? Did this event stir guilt or shame? Did I, for a moment, feel as though I had no control over my experience, much like in the previous situation? These are some questions to consider when you find yourself provoked.

So What, What Then, and Then What

The *So What, What Then, and Then What*—used in any order or combination—is one of my favorite tried-and-true methods for restoration. I implement this sequence several times a week with clients who deal with anxiety tied to the unknown, fears, imaginations, and all things unsettling. To ease into it, I ask if I've ever used the *So What, What Then, and Then What* technique with them—most of the time, they don't remember.

I pose a question that feels overwhelming in their mind—one that can stir anxiety and fear. As an example, let's consider a woman who confesses that she struggles with a strong fear of what others may think about her in the workplace. The inquiry goes like this:

Me: So if you're in the breakroom and two co-workers are in there but do not greet you, what then?

Josie: Well then I would feel scared!

Me: So then what?

Josie: Well, my feelings would be hurt.

Me: And what then?

Josie: I would feel bad and cry.

Me: And then what?

Josie: Then I would stop crying.

At that moment Josie realizes that her fear and anxiety were based on her own unconfronted imaginations. This situation held the weight of authority because she had accepted that it would be extremely painful if someone did not acknowledge her. While these ideas remained overpowering in her mind, once she began to voice them and corner them with the *So What, What Then, and Then What* questions, they lost their credibility, and she found herself laughing.

Self-Forgiveness

Let's talk about the hard stuff—when you do have some genuine ownership of your past choices and mistakes. There may be times when some circumstances could have been different had other choices been made. While not everything is within your control, there may be moments where your decisions played a role. This is not about blame, but about honest reflection. For example, suppose your child was abused and you didn't leave the relationship soon enough. Of course, I would guide you through self-forgiveness, as there are often significant psychological, emotional, and situational obstacles at play in cases like this. I use this extreme example to help you, the reader, understand that there may be deep regrets you carry—and that is understandable.

In a session like this, I affirm the feelings of guilt, and yes, I acknowledge the sense of failure. I verbalize that I can understand why you'd feel the weight of neglect and culpability. Accusation, however, is never part of the approach. I recognize that if an individual is already naming their mistakes, there is likely enough internal criticism taking place. Simply admitting responsibility provides plenty to work with.

It is important for me to acknowledge one's sense of responsibility; otherwise, the mind may begin searching for loopholes, interpreting any denial of the experience as an omission of truth, which can interfere with progress. To understand this further, the mind often looks for consistency and meaning, trying to organize and make sense of a person's experiences. If I were to deny that a particular choice carried responsibility, it could create a sense of incongruence, leading to resistance rather than movement toward healing.

Accepting that you can forgive yourself for your errors is not something that is typically embraced on the first attempt. I often have to circle back in different ways to help disarm guarded beliefs. This is a process. In the same way, you may find yourself needing to revisit certain exercises more than once to reach a place of forgiveness. Remember, without self-forgiveness, you may remain in your unresolved wounds.

Small Progress, Significant Change

When we are the ones navigating personal turmoil, and it is all we have known, we count progress differently than those on the outside. I express great pride in those individuals I serve when they take the first step to talk about the trauma their past left behind. They need to hear, through an objective perspective, that their first step truly does have an immediate impact.

Acknowledging growth and change, even in small amounts, rewires the brain. We want more and more of this effect because it is through these moments that you begin to believe that small is great, and great is significant. Nothing should go uncounted when it is costing you effort to move forward. Remember, there are people in this world who are at least one step behind you because they have not chosen to move forward at all.

Adopt the habit of counting progress daily. Become addicted to it. It is a form of renewing your mind. Most of us overlook small progress because we are fixated on how much more work we have ahead of us.

It is not rare that when I celebrate too loudly, some of my clients will insist that they still have a long road ahead of them. This occurs because they have formed a connection with me and are afraid to lose it too quickly, but the other half of this is that they don't want to accept the gains too quickly, as it rejects the beliefs they have been living through for many years. Even when something is not healthy, we can still struggle with letting some things go. Remember, as you lay in bed, learn from the failures, count the changes.

Sticky Notes

Like many other excellent and compassionate mental health practitioners, I develop a deep love and care for my clients. We learn to truly appreciate each one of them and often connect over a particular experience they've shared—an ultra-vulnerable moment—and sometimes we join hearts over humor. My habit is to always meet them where they are and help them get where they want to be, and even further.

In one particular session with one of my funniest clients, I shared a comment that really impacted them. At that moment, they gestured with their fingers and exclaimed, "STICKY NOTE!" Now, every time there is a mind-shifting statement, that is our official "sticky note!" moment. I want to share this sticky note tidbit with you.

I am certain you will find sticky note statements as you turn the pages. One statement or reminder has the power to reinforce changes in your thinking patterns, which in turn can change your life. Whether you literally use those fun little yellow adhesive squares, a note in your phone, a journal, or even a dry-erase marker on your bathroom mirror, an intentional prompt is a tool for your toolkit.

Look for the Evidence

If there was ever a powerful metaphor that could contribute to nearly all of the thinking you carry, it is this one: Imagine looking for the evidence in everything you believe, not just for reparation's sake. As you investigate the evidence in your thought processes, you confront the beliefs that are influencing and enforcing a large part of your life.

Imagine making decisions day in and day out based on something you have believed, but never challenged against the evidence. As you have analyzed your fault-finding statements, I trust you have found a release—one that will carry you into the next season of your life with a new perspective and train you to question the ideas you accept as truth.

These narrative shifts can be as simple as feeling like you never do anything right. In that case, I would have a client describe their day to me from the beginning up to the point of our appointment. The account would contain details about waking up, showering, picking out an outfit, cooking breakfast, maybe taking their child to school. I would then inquire if they liked the outfit they are wearing. Most of the time, they would answer, "Yes." I would proceed with a simple, "Okay, so you did at least one thing right." I would (perhaps annoyingly) continue to ask about their breakfast. Did they burn their food I wonder? No, not typically. There is a second thing they did right.

This is so simple it is nearly trivial. These examples, however, are powerful demonstrations that pierce deep into the seemingly simple places that define a large portion of our thought life.

The Empathy Principle

I believe compassion and empathy are a decision, but also a heart posture which is learned in the childhood years, or acquired through hardship or exposure to certain situations. I have witnessed a surge of individuals merging into the mental health field just to "see how it goes." They did not necessarily feel a call to this, but thought they would give it a go since they were bored with their current career. On the other hand, others have jumped in and found what they have been missing all along. This work, my friends, is a calling. It provides the grace to get through the many stories that you will hear day after day with no end in sight. It also provides the capacity to leave those accounts at the office no matter how burdensome they felt to your heart while they shared.

Empathy will keep you from minimizing someone's story, even if you feel it is small, or if you realize that many others have gone through much worse. A strong practitioner understands that being able to engage with various levels of detriment is stronger because of it.

I understand why a helping practitioner may be tempted to ascribe their inner stance to certain experiences, but clients do not heal by what someone else has endured; they recover by what we acknowledge and do not minimize. Once the validation process takes place, the tears have been cried, and the heart's burdens have been released, the nervous system finds its calm. Only then can problem solving and integration begin.

Fix Your Face

I have spent years training leaders, especially in the faith community, in dealing with the weary of mind and heart. I like to remind the learners, and this applies to all backgrounds, that they may hear some of the most unbelievable accounts—some downright inhumane. And that when an individual has entrusted their ears to hear, they must provide a secure environment and should "fix their face."

Care providers may be hesitant to admit that they have to work hard at keeping their thoughts and facial expressions in check. I won't! I will keep it real and say that from time to time, you will realize you have not heard it all. Empathy trains you that your face does not have to say everything you are thinking. Even if it is reasonable and justified, some facial and verbal responses could hinder instead of help. Since the person sitting in the healing chair is already in a vulnerable state, often against their surface level wishes, this could invite shame. I admit this may sound extreme, but those who are carrying burdens beyond what we understand at face value, overanalyze and can show signs of hypervigilance when unveiling details that have been stored away.

You Cannot Heal What You Withhold Compassion From

Exactly how does this portion of the book relate to you if you are seeking the healing, and not necessarily reading it as a practitioner? It is an imperative portion. In the same way I am describing the various events that others experienced, so I am preparing you to extend compassion to your own life's circumstances. You may be tempted to rationalize your own unresolved encounters and convince yourself that they are not a big deal, or in need of clinical, therapeutic, or reparation labeling. You may deny yourself the time to sit and sift through your memory box, rushing a transformation path because you have decided it does not deserve the attention and focus.

Empathy is not optional; it is essential. The posture you take toward yourself will either deepen or diminish what you encounter here. Decide now that the voice of self-reprimand will not accompany you through these pages.

Claiming My Pain, Protecting My Loved Ones

A very common defense mechanism known as *rationalization* is one of the most common behaviors that human beings quickly deploy during a healing session. That is because participants hold a strong belief that acknowledging the pain that their loved ones contributed to their lives means they are betraying them and not recognizing them for the good things they did. My protocol is to warn the recipients ahead of time. "We are not blaming, we are identifying. I am simply looking for behaviors," I advise. Once I lay that out, they begin to relax and their brain begins to put down its need to alert and protect them from my words and influence. From time to time, I may have to repeat it again within a few minutes, but not typically much after that.

We often feel deep guilt when we speak honestly about our experiences regarding family. This is especially true when those experiences challenge the belief that our family members and loved ones were only capable of good. We are human, and every one of us has the capacity to do both good and harm to one another. When we enter into the space of memory—where details are stored in the brain—and are able to revisit a painful recollection, it becomes possible to reshape the emotional residue it left behind. Without the willingness to go back there, some events, thoughts, and memories may remain unprocessed and feel as though they are held hostage.

This can be very common with an individual who was raised by one parent alone. Often, their entire loyalty is committed to that particular parental figure for the care, sacrifice, time, and provision they contributed to their lives. But this does not deny that there were also activities, behaviors, choices, or patterns that left a dent in the heart.

Moving forward from this to the healing journey is learning to differentiate between identifying and blaming. Blaming keeps grace arrested and leaves no room for others to redeem their mistakes and wrongdoings. It says their intentions were without a doubt deliberately malicious, and I refuse them an opening to fix or heal their errors. Identifying says: I recognize that though I loved them very much, they were able to miss the mark, and that affected me. I realize they may have meant well, but perfection was impossible, and it etched pain within me. Now I want to pinpoint the broken pieces, so that I can detect its effects in my present day.

There are a few exceptions where genuinely destroying who you were could have been the aim, but those cases are few. And while they are few, they are still real nonetheless. For the sake of this book, we will assume that their intentions were good, but failure was inevitable.

PROCESS WITH ME

Throughout my sessions, I provide an invitation for clients to engage in a powerful way with what has been said. I open the door for them to express what they are feeling, thinking, accepting, rejecting, and healing up to that point of the meeting.

They talk, I respond, then they solidify. You, my friend, will partake in the same process.

Through this book, you have access to the same tools I offer to those I visit with in person or virtually. You don't have to "punch the air" alone, as my youngest son calls it when he is wrestling with his innermost thoughts. What *Process With Me* offers is a guided healing journey, and every piece is carefully structured with you in mind. Whether in person or through these pages, your well being is my aspiration.

If you've noticed, I've used several words to describe the processing blueprint, although it is not a comprehensive list. Each of these words, however, describes the potential mental and emotional repositioning that acts like the glue for new things discovered. Nothing will anchor without the reflective portion of what you say out loud.

For the full experience, you will need something to write with and document. Use your phone, a journal, a notepad, or any other instrument of your choice. My preference will always be a pen and paper because it utilizes greater brain power.

To begin, I have several guidelines to help make your experience memorable and more effective. First, whatever you write in, treat it as sacred. In other words, it should not be your son's graded worksheet that was sent home for parental review, a marketing piece that came in the mail, or some random sheet that will be trashed. Keep in mind that healing is costly in every way. It costs you emotional and mental fatigue, physical overexertion due to things passing through and letting loose. Guard it as such.

Date everything! As a woman who has been through several seasons of healing myself, it is exciting to look back at a particular journal entry and reminisce on where I have been and how far I have come. These are reinforcements to your recovery.

Take your time when journaling. No rushing. If you find yourself hastening through, stop and ask yourself, "What am I avoiding?" Is the feeling beginning to overtake your reality at that moment? If so, stop, breathe, and remind yourself that you have full control and are no longer at the mercy of the events or people that harmed you. Once you give yourself a moment of grace and reset, start again. Remember that your brain is trying to protect you from "feeling" those events again, so it distracts you. It wants to avoid the energy it would require to get you well because it just wants to "keep you safe." But the false sense of safety may be delaying the greatness sitting on the other side of that momentary feeling.

Write as much as you can because your restoration depends on it. Write in detail; use descriptive words, because writing *is* the "talking about it" portion. Relate the cadence of the experience. One of the signs of trauma is the limited expression of feelings. Some of this has to be walked out and worked through entry by entry and exercise by exercise.

Stop every couple of paragraphs as needed, take a breath, then read what you have out loud. The more you write and speak, the more opportunity you are providing for the brain to become what is known as malleable, meaning flexible and collaborative. This will even reframe the meaning of how you once interpreted a thing, and it is now able to redefine the hefty meaning of all your experiences. It can reduce them to merely memories and experiences, instead of threats. Memories untreated become one of the first filters of all your experiences. This, my friend, is why a specific behavior from an unpleasant individual from the past will be likened to another person who repeats a pattern that is even seemingly similar, even if they are part of a pleasant relationship .

In conclusion, please do not judge or label the encounters, details, and thoughts that go through your mind prematurely. One commonly utilized statement voiced by clients is, "I know this is stupid, but..." To label your thoughts as stupid is to reinforce the very things we are attempting to see you healed from. Be detailed and unafraid. Once you begin to move those fingers on paper and open that mouth, the disarming begins!

I Remove Your Permission

Much like the prior piece of advice, you might also hear me say, "I remove your permission to..." I may say, I remove your permission to say yes to a man that keeps knocking at your door with no intentions to be there for you, or I remove your permission to say those words to yourself again. For those who want to heal, this is an accountability statement they will hear in their heads when they encounter those moments that feed the state they are in at the time.

This is doing for you what you cannot do for yourself. You would be surprised at the people that just need someone they trust to simply say, "No more!" Usually, it's no more saying yes to people who use you, constantly disrespect you even if it's family, and no to anything that assaults your value, ability to heal, and self-respect.

No Shortcuts

Up to this point, you may have only read a short portion of the work I put into this project, and that is perfectly fine. I strongly advise against taking shortcuts and selecting preferred sections to tackle. Once you have navigated through the entirety of the book once, skip away!

I have a special friend who loves to skip to the chapters she thinks may be the best in the entire book. We laugh at her habits, as they are not harmful, but in this case, don't do it! I have had to do that myself, but this book is not that. The pieces do work together in the order that I have written them. That is because every portion of this internal navigation guide has its purpose, and that is how they will be most effective. Step into the journey that gave birth to this book.

3

A WORD TO THOSE WHO HELP OTHERS HEAL

Outside of counseling, I have been doing public speaking for years, but I remember one of my first and most important speaking events completely flopping because I was so nervous. I was deeply disappointed in myself for allowing anxiety to take over. Although I was one hundred percent prepared for my presentation, I was not prepared for the intimidation I sensed. I allowed myself to be guided by what I was experiencing, not by the purpose and goal of my being there.

Once that event was over, I analyzed, scrutinized, and criticized my performance, but I made a decision: I would never again allow myself to be overtaken by nervousness or negativity. From that point forward, I resolved to treat every single event as if it were my one and only chance to say what I needed to say in that moment. That approach has become how I live most of my life now. I remind myself that every encounter with a hurting individual may be the only opportunity I ever have to impact their life—so I treat them as people first, and clients second. Compassion and empathy must meet them at the door, along with warmth and joy.

Intake forms and questionnaires are important, but they will never matter if help-seekers do not experience your compassion. Imagine this: these individuals woke up to face life, and for some, they barely made it—if you know what I mean. They got ready for work, and at some point remembered they had an appointment with you. They have been wondering about who you are. Interestingly, most are not thinking about where you completed your graduate studies. They are wondering whether you will see them, understand them, and help them navigate life's most pressing questions with an objective stance.

It is very likely, as I hear on a daily basis, that help-seekers experience anxiety simply in anticipation of their scheduled session. Many are lost, scared, and desperately hopeful, but also afraid of disappointment. Their concerns surround them as they wonder whether they will be judged for their deepest thoughts, fears, hang-ups, and beliefs.

Being who you are, in this line of work, automatically increases the likelihood in their mind that you may be the person they have been waiting for. You may even be their second or third attempt at finding help, hoping this time will be different—that they will finally forge a connection with another human being who understands life. Show up as if you are their one and only opportunity in that moment to move out of those imagined or very real dark places.

Another motto I live by and use to train leaders and lay counselors is: "I am real, vulnerable, and transparent." These three principles, when applied, will change how others respond to you. You can carry them anywhere and apply them in almost any setting. Please do not misunderstand me—it does not mean I disclose everything about my life to those under my care. Rather, I am not afraid to share stories that create connection if they help someone feel less alone in their pain and process. I share what I choose to share, and I allow others to see my humanity as well.

How are you applying these principles in your professional relationships? Would you want to sit with yourself if you were the one seeking help? Would your clients refer you to their friends and loved ones? Would they leave feeling hopeful and significantly better than when they arrived? I often hear the grumblings from others navigating the challenges of human behavior who say, "People are being peoplely." But that phrase can be reframed with a positive twist: Let's be more peoplely.

Healer, Do You Trust Thyself?

Another principle of effective healing begins with being fully convinced that souls in search of wholeness will sense if they can trust you, and whether or not you trust yourself. They scan for the empathy principle immediately, and when things feel solely mechanical, they may not progress at all, and even worse, they may not return. Mechanical says, "They don't even know themselves." It points to a disconnection within the healing technician that clients will not miss.

One reality to consider is that even with the most rigorous, science-backed interventions and documentation, outcomes may still reflect only minimal gains. We can prove this by the many conversations individuals have day in and day out with a familiar person or even a stranger. They come out of those social encounters with a sense of "I needed that."

I have heard endless reports from clients that some practitioners show up with a little "checklist" to counsel. Others have reported that their facilitators would constantly look at their watch, or even place blame on the client for their failing pieces instead of walking them through a self-discovery path that could have promoted ownership.

Aligning with my shared pillars sets the stage for those entrusted to you to begin opening up and working through the profoundly strained places of their mind, soul, and memories. Not long after, they begin to break free from what has been constraining them.

I believe everyone in the helping field has a right to develop and own what works for them, and the wise acknowledge that this is an ever-evolving skill, and we learn something new every day. Adjustments should take place as needed, but empathy, compassion, and trust are requirements now. For some of you, life has already activated these superpowers within you. If not, life itself will take you for a spin and train you through the school of hard knocks.

Section 2

Disarming What Gets in the Way

4

THE WALK TOWARD SOMETHING GREAT

It was the year 2015, and the day was nice, warm, and sunny. I still remember this particular day as if it happened a few weeks ago. I was wearing my black and pink shorts and my running shoes, and my friend Liz and I were out for a run. That day, we were sharing our dreams regarding our education and career goals. As I shared with my friend that, in my much younger years, I wanted to be a psychologist or counselor, she jumped on board and said, "You should do it!" Liz is really good at egging on all my crazy, wild ideas no matter the cost. Within minutes of sharing the dream of long ago, it only took one person to dare me, and there I was registered for my first master's level counseling course.

In a short amount of time, I graduated with my degree in professional counseling and passed my National Counselor

Examination. Well, it wasn't as easy as I am making it out to be, but with a few months of studying, crying, stressing, and trusting, I completed this process. It was completely worth it, no doubt.

It is also important to note that prior to entering the professional counseling field, I had already been working with individuals in pastoral counseling and executive coaching since 2009, and at that point I had helped hundreds of people. The professional counseling field would allow me to further develop my clinical training while continuing the work I had already been providing within those dynamic spaces.

Fast forward ten years later to October 2025. There we were, Liz and I, walking at the park. This time I was sharing with her that I wanted to write a book on a counseling topic. Although I had been mulling over this idea before I arrived at the park, I still wasn't sure what the topic would be. I knew I wanted it to be something that empowered individuals to talk about issues with more confidence, as I have witnessed the battles people face in opening up. As we walked and talked, and I shared my frustrations on certain loosely related issues, suddenly the download began and I had a title, and seconds later, the subtitle of this book: *Talk About It: Healing the Trauma That Your Past Left Behind!* We were both elated. The smile on her face showed agreement, and I was so excited to know that the topic and title were both inspired at that very moment.

An Unexpected Direction

This isn't the first book I have written, but I never imagined that I would write a book on trauma, even though I am in the mental health and healing practice. Sure, I believe in restoration from trauma. I work with it daily, without fail. Many of the individuals I have consulted through various healing platforms have often been tormented with the residual symptoms of one or more tragic events. Yet I would have naturally leaned toward writing a book on completely different topics—something more touchy-feely.

Most of the time I can respect science that has been proven, but I love dealing with soul issues through a more spiritual approach. And as I continued to encounter countless individuals who have spent time with me through guidance and coaching sessions, there was a constant—nearly all were living through the symptoms of trauma. Whether through experiences of sexual, physical, or verbal abuse, violence, freak accidents, death, divorce, or sickness, they were all afraid to confront this one thing: fear of talking about it. This fear keeps the trauma alive, active, and unhealed. The issue is that much of what they feared was largely imagined and stored in their brain and body.

A client's idea of reliving the moment of devastation through talking felt like living it for the first time again. Their apprehension nearly shut them down and kept them from crossing over to the healthier side of things. But then, they took a small step—maybe even only spoke around the dreaded topic—and the light began to shine for them mentally and internally. Now I hope to shine that light for you.

Little Therapist

While the decision to continue my education was made on a sunny day at the park, the days of giving advice for life started when I was only a young girl. I hadn't yet developed the skills to brush my hair well, but there I was spouting out encouragement that seemed to satisfy the littles looking for direction. What *exactly* was it that I was suggesting is still fully unknown to me, but I started to become aware, even back then, that I attracted hurting people, and I was drawn by the need to solve problems and to witness hope arise in them again.

I vividly remember talking to one of my first "counseling" clients when I was no more than 10 years of age. We will call my first client Daniella. Daniella was around 12 years old and fought with her mom all the time. She was upset that her mom was not willing to trust her around friends in fear that she was making unhealthy choices. For mom, it wasn't just an imagination. Family and friends around Daniella had been reporting the poor choices she was making when mom was not around. Indignant at the lack of trust, Daniella scoffed at her mom's audacity, and felt judged and misunderstood. I began to share my advice on how she could host a successful conflict resolution meeting with mom to win her over. That is when Daniella encouraged me to become a counselor one day, and she felt relieved to have had someone to download her stress to, who could offer principles of resolution. I remember realizing at that moment that this is what counselors did—they listened and advised.

Now thirty something years later, I am often overcome with awe when I think that I get paid to have amazing conversations with people! OK, it's more than that when you break it down—it is gaining trust and sharing principles that heal. Counseling, guidance, healing, coaching—it's like helping clients find puzzle pieces and putting them together to make them make sense, while helping them attain direction and healing to the secrets of their hearts.

There is a weighted feeling that drops into my heart, or often surges from deep places as I witness people marvel at their breakthrough. That is, the moment when they experience something they never thought would be possible – the ability to *talk about* the untold story they have been holding captive due to shame, blame, embarrassment, or minimization of its importance. Even at a young age I was able to discern that *look* a person gets when the *aha* moment unveils. It's a mix between relief and *what just happened?*

Countless recipients of healing were sure no one would be able to crack the self-imposed or societal expectation of staying in bondage to their past and pain. But I always have been and will be their number one cheerleader as they heal. This compassion which is embedded with a history of results has increased my determination to yell from the rooftops that if you just talk about it, your healing is at a conversation's length. As long as the conversation happens with someone who understands the journey of pain and healing as an individual, not just from a textbook, you should find relief. Even then, dialogue with any non-judgmental individual can make room for alleviation.

Prepare, Train, Trust

One of my most repeated gems is "Intention is everything." And that is the truth. To prepare your mind and body, including your brain, to join in this life-giving journey, I have to actively prepare you to intentionally invest yourself fully. I want your mind–that which consists of the life force of reasoning, understanding, perceiving, and thinking–to align with, and put your brain at ease, so it can enter into the self journey of talking about the trauma.

Anytime we are about to make a decision, the brain scans for the file that informs it, helping you determine whether to participate in that decision. Take for example, the following scenario: It's a lovely day outside, and the day is just right. You begin to toss around the idea of going to the bookstore. For a few seconds, the idea seems good. You almost have your shoes on, when all of the sudden a mist of funk and weight begins to settle on you. All of the sudden you *feel* overwhelmed. You begin to "think" that putting on your shoes may actually be too much work after all. The thoughts and feelings progress, but your imagination is also at work with the mind and your body. At this point you received the traffic report in your head, and, well, no one likes to get stuck on the highway and street lights. To seal the deal, you have also decided finding a parking spot is just too much for a weekday.

Recognize what just happened. An imagination activated your mind, followed by the brain, and eventually the body. This all happens at rapid speed. What could have been a healthy, much-needed outing, was now a burden so heavy, that even the body opted out. This is the power of intention and imagination.

As soon as you hear the words healing, mental health, trauma, counseling, emotional processing, and the like, it may shut you down. Why? Because you *imagined* it through the lens of a negative expectation and experience. What if I led you through a positive scenario regarding the bookstore? You might want to go shopping as late as midnight!

Only Imagine: Engaging The Mind, The Brain, and The Body

Once we get the mind and brain on board, we bring the body into the experience as well. To begin—*Only Imagine*. The goal of this section is to set a foundation for seeing, hearing, and sensing only positive images of the healed version of you.

Imagine your face for a minute—you have the Sunday best smile. Your makeup is perfect, or you are well-shaven. Your complexion speaks of your healthy eating habits. You no longer carry the trauma-heavy countenance of fear and worry that most people exude when the unprocessed and undiscovered hidden layers of the *secrets not said* exist.

Your eyes are glowing, like a fire. They communicate that destructive thoughts, troubling recollections, beliefs, and imaginations have been evicted—for good. What is left is a glow of hope and expectation. You are now capable of receiving compliments without your heart beating fast, and your blood rushing to your head. Instead, it feels like a kiss from heaven.

Your hair is salon-grade and professionally pampered. The clothing on your body finally looks fitting, and it's evident it was carefully chosen. You feel great!

To top off that ensemble, your heart is finally light, and you're experiencing a peace you were convinced never existed for people who have experienced events like yours. You look to the left and right, as if you are searching for something that has been with you for many years. Only it cannot be found—anxiety. Instead of that dreaded symptom, you feel your heart leap with excitement. About what? No reason! Your core knows better is coming just because you exist on the earth.

The level of fatigue is now converted to energy, and you enjoy taking brisk walks. You feel that? The warm sun is hitting your arms. The birds quietly chirp as if they're welcoming you. The tree branches softly dance for you with a warm welcome.

All is well with the world. Those you deeply care about are taken care of. The bills are paid. You have some play money, but the greatest gift in your possession is your peace of mind. Now breathe! And, breathe again.

Check In with Your Experience

How did you feel through this exercise? Did you begin to feel a release of useless weight? Were you feeling a bit more hopeful and positive? Were you able to hone in on the birds, trees, and sun on your arms? Was there some other experience you were encountering that assisted in creating a readiness to take on the deeper topics?

The Power of Imagination

Imagining is a powerful tool. I can make myself want or be repelled by something simply by imagining what I believe about a particular thing. Take truffles or cilantro, for example. I have heard that people either love them or hate them, and that there is no in-between. If I never smelled truffles again, life would be even better. I can imagine myself sick thinking about them. Cilantro, on the other hand—let's put a little on eggs, tacos, beans, even a hot dog.

What you imagine will work for you if you allow it. Leading your mind, brain, and body into a positive imaginary exercise can set you up to deconstruct the dread that you imagine processing trauma may be. I often ask my clients if they were dreading our session in fear of what we would encounter during that day's session. My response is usually a gentle giggle or a smile to help reassure them that all will be well, followed by a series of questions that break apart the stronghold of anxiety or fear of talking about it.

A Glimpse into Healing Conversations

Head's up, I am a Southern-Latina woman who loves Jesus, and I call people "honey" or "love" as a term of endearment. I realize some may huff at the idea of it, but unless my clients are offended, it goes something like this:

Me: So, honey, talk to me about our last session. What was the worst part of visiting the details and the memories of the past?

Client: Thinking about how hard it was going to be.

Me: OK. That makes sense. Was it as hard as you imagined?

Client: No, but I wasn't looking forward to it.

Me: I hear you. I can see why you would feel that way. So, what are some positive things about the trauma processing that you want to share with me?

Client: Honestly, I felt relieved. Like I was finally validated. Then I felt really tired for a couple of days.

Me: Did the anxiety alleviate some?

Client: Yes, I am not thinking about it as much right before I go to sleep.

Me: Great, so you are saying that the experience was actually positive, with desirable results, and the hardest part was what you imagined it would be like versus what actually occurred?

Client: Yes, but I am still not looking forward to it.

Me: I understand. The thing is, we have to repeat this process a few times for your brain to record that healing is a good thing, and talking about it is actually how we get there. It needs to understand that you are safe, you are in control today, and what happened to you back then will never happen again.

This is a very short but general idea of what my clients report after talking about it. Eventually, they begin to seek out that particular experience and realize the effects they once had pre-processing are no longer present, and they wonder if they are even healing since the adrenaline rush no longer activates when they are sharing the details of their dreaded circumstances.

In other words, healing can become addicting, and there is nothing wrong with that. Only, imagine yourself healed before taking yourself through any steps of healing, and imagine the truth—that healing is your desire.

5

TRAUMA: WHY WE DON'T TALK ABOUT IT AND WHY WE SHOULD

Pain is one of humanity's greatest fears. We ardently dread visiting the process of past turmoil and often avoid it at all costs. It's rare that I meet anyone who willingly submitted themselves to receiving help for their past torments, but just the right unexpected circumstance triggered them into a corner, unfolding a trauma erupting session. In other words, they lost their crap and then held regrets for the outburst. It's in those moments that they unwantedly leaked their inner mess all over the place.

The preventative measure would have been to *Talk About It!* To discuss it with a trusted, qualified professional, friend, trained spiritual leader, or other solid source. The ideal healing circumstance would provide a trusted space that leaves no room for judgment or over-opinionated solutions. Put simply, a place to land—where anger is allowed, tears are welcome, and the unrestrained soul can finally exhale. A place where even the face speaks, and emotion gives testimony to the shame of what occurred in the past or even the recent present.

My focus will remain on making talking about it a healthy norm. This is not to be confused with trauma dumping, but with addressing trauma in a productive setting—the trauma our past has left behind.

Speaking of trauma dumping...

The Truth About Trauma Dumping - And How This Is Different

Now, some of you may be a bit confused, especially if you tend to go around "trauma dumping" and telling it all, everywhere you go. That means dropping everything like it is hot, no matter where you are. You tell everyone about your momma, daddy, cousins, and everyone in between, as if saying it out loud alone is enough to heal the million little pieces of your heart.

The truth is, trauma dumping is nothing but a detached way to tell your story to anyone who will listen while it provides a false sense of healing or of being healed. This behavior simply allows you to tell your story without truly binding up the bleeding wounds. I am not saying that every time you share *anything* you are trauma dumping, of course not! I share a lot of my story on various platforms, but I share a very processed version of my past.

In reality, your soul is crying out for the answers and seeking an understanding of what occurred. You may even unknowingly lay out the personal portions in hope that someone will get you, and answer you with something that will make sense and put your heart at ease. The portions of my past people get to hear about are generally the ones I have spoken out loud to a trusted, qualified individual. These are the segments that have had the impurities removed from them, omitting any attached unhealthy meaning to my suffering.

Trauma healing occurs best when the sacred portions of your story are told to a trustworthy person, in a confidential space, where grace, compassion, and processing can happen all at the same time. However, since you may not make room for someone who can help you through this in person, I will take you through various fractions and steps of what I do to help people become whole when they sit for a one-on-one talk, or even a group or public session.

Initial Expectations, Resistances, Fears, and Hopes

So why don't we freely share the events and memories that haunt us? The answer has many pieces, but summed up, it's very simple—fear. Fear that retelling even one portion might awaken the shame we've so neatly folded away in the pile labeled *"will never be seen again."* We cling to the false belief that if it's ignored, it might simply disappear and heal itself. Fear that if we share the details out loud, it will feel exactly like it did that particular day when the disturbing events emerged.

We dread allowing the people involved in those trauma inducing moments into our memories once again—sensing their essence, seeing the look in their eyes, hearing the sounds, and smelling the air or the environment where these episodes transpired. We attempt to avoid experiencing how time slowed when the hell broke loose, and there was no one to chase the moments away.

At this point of my career I have counseled, guided, and coached hundreds of people, and can assure you that nearly every single one of them that was haunted by the *idea* of talking about it in the end felt an enormous amount of relief, and as a result, healed. These individuals were relieved to realize that the mere imagination of talking about tragic events in their past could not hurt them again.

Those who avoid the healing will, in time, face the unavoidable. At some unpredictable moment they may risk publicly or privately experiencing any of the following symptoms which are part of unresolved trauma:

- Anxiety
- Fear or panic
- Sadness or depression
- Guilt or shame
- Anger or irritability
- Feeling emotionally numb or detached

Mental Symptoms

- Trouble concentrating or remembering
- Confusion or disorientation
- Flashbacks or intrusive memories
- Nightmares
- Constant vigilance or hyper-awareness

Physical Symptoms

- Headaches or tension
- Fatigue or muscle pain
- Rapid heartbeat or palpitations
- Digestive issues
- Sleep disturbances
- Changes in appetite or energy

Behavioral Symptoms

- Avoiding reminders of the trauma
- Social withdrawal or isolation
- Substance use and abuse to cope
- Risky behaviors or self-harm
- Difficulty maintaining relationships

I can hear my readers thinking, "Everyone I know experiences these symptoms." And while it may appear so, the person carrying unresolved distress is still set apart from the rest. Once you meet an individual with active trauma, you will understand how they differ. They carry a sort of a double-edged sword whereby they shift between fragility and a boiling over.

For example, two of the most common but possibly overlooked trauma symptoms by everyday people are irritability and agitation. Recovering drug users may even testify to this and tell you that they live in a state of emotional reactivity such as annoyance or frustration, thus pointing to irritability or agitation, with the inability to feel calm in their body. Without diving into complex science, the key takeaway is that your emotions are grounded in biology, meaning in the body, not just the mind and heart, and understanding this can help you engage with your experiences more effectively.

A statement that I coined and share in my office or in virtual sessions many times a day is, "The soul demands healing." When I speak of the soul, I am talking about that which contains the mind, the will, the emotions, and the intellect—in essence, the life force of much of who you are. Just like the body expressing unresolved emotional pain through sickness, so will the tormented soul express itself through untamable outbursts, eruptions, or even trouble sleeping.

Talking Is Not Reliving

Someone needs to tell you that the pain of reliving the moment and memory of that particular dread is not the same as the *actual* event. The imagination has blown it up to protect you from what it has defined as danger. Your brain is doing what it is supposed to, just not at the *right time*. But there is no need to protect against what is not going to occur again, assuming you have left the harmful environment or context. Today you more than likely are under different circumstances.

Maybe you are not in the same country you were in when the trauma occurred, or work at the same job, or are married to the same person. Maybe you are not in the same general location, or are now an adult and can protect yourself unlike when you were a little person with no control. Think about it. What do you have control over today regarding your situation that you did not have control over back then? Some traumatic intensity is broken by making a decision to evaluate what is and is not still true.

Imagining, writing, and verbally rehearsing the opposite of the imaginations that control you is often a miraculous endeavor for healing. But how will you know to do this if no one has told you that this does work, and has worked for others?

Resistance: Holding onto Control

Resistance can be seen as a form of control. As backwards as it may sound, some people will say with their mouth that they would like to heal, but their actions relate a different message. One way to look at this is to identify the resistance as a form of control. Human beings practice this behavior at all times of their lives, and letting go of what they know is not healthy, to welcome the good, does not automatically cause them to release the hold. Keep in mind that your brain is controlling much of the resistance, which means you must make up your mind (a part of the soul) to get your brain to cooperate.

I have had men and women show up to their appointments in a visibly foul mood. During periods of resistance one may experience anger, frustration, weepiness, and a general sense of intense emotions, but the wall is always the leading position. As a woman who has sat on the same side of every person who has sought help and healing, I can attest that this feeling is very real, and can present itself when least expected, but it *will* get in your way.

As you journey through these pages and if you begin to feel overwhelmed, angry, agitated, or intensely emotional, put the book down momentarily. Consider if you may be in a state of resistance. Begin to question and gently confront the fears presenting themselves as resistance. Ask yourself: What am I so afraid of? Do I believe I am in danger by entering into this moment of emotional surrender? What is the worst that can really happen by reliving these moments other than the discomfort of the stored experiences?

As you attempt to expose the fears and mental misinformation, sound beliefs begin to surface, allowing you to continue in the process. If the trauma locked in proves to be extremely intense, this will be a bit more challenging. And if this is the case, I would prompt you to take small pieces at a time. After all, what's the rush? Most people have been hosting these events and memories for so long, a bit longer is sustainable as you extend grace toward your movement forward.

Not all fear of losing control is an overreaction. Vulnerability in the past may have been the culprit for many harmful encounters, so the mind and the brain resist releasing control. Exercising the courage to let go is the key to much healing. Remember that the power is in your hands now, not the event, not even the circumstances or those who were once involved in your situation.

The Unanswerable Why

Much like your soul demands healing, your heart demands answers. It wants to know the "why." It insists on finding causation that will soothe the aching inner core. It believes that if we locate an explanation, all will be well with our world. In reality, even with a logical account, it may never satisfy the search because pain doesn't always accept the rationale. It may only be the start of never-ending grasping for more of the same—"Why?"

In reality this only fortifies the trauma stored up within ourselves, including the brain. It continues to send a signal to the whole person reminding us that something is unsettled. At what point will the pause in your restoration be long enough? What if you never find a satisfactory reason for what happened to you or your loved one? Will you lose years of your life, joy that could be accessed, relationships that could be forged if you were to receive a restoration regardless of the reason behind it?

It's painful, I know. It hurts to soul search and find emptiness that only intensifies the burning and confusion when our mind has nothing to reach to. It's almost like starting all over again. Hear what I just said. As you reach, you reignite. It is important to state that the brain desperately seeks to find information that is logical so it can move on from that moment. As I often say to my clients, "The brain is always looking for a landing place."

Can I encourage you to set your nervous system free and give up the hunt when appropriate? The very act of releasing triggers an alert in the brain, signaling that if you let go of this, you are vulnerable. In a normal circumstance, the brain kicking in to protect you is acceptable and what is supposed to occur. But when you are attempting to let go of a reason to feel vindicated for any event that wounded you, it can feel like danger itself. Still, you have the power to retrain your mind, your brain, and your body.

Those who want to be healed, set free, and unburdened from life's heaviest loads will begin to disarm the brain from feeling threatened. You as a person must begin to make the choice to release the right to have a reason for the past mess. Once you decide from your mind—the place where the seat of your emotions, life's appetites, and reasoning reside—the rest of your being follows.

Make the decision and begin to intentionally tell your brain what to conclude. In this case, you will consciously practice thinking that you are safe to release the need to have understanding and answers for your sufferings and demise in order to move forward in your restoration journey. Of course, this may take several times to master, but it can work if you utilize the methods.

Why It's Not Your Fault, Even When it Feels Like it is

Humanity has an exemplary gift of taking false responsibility for traumatizing events, yet often neglects the truth that brings healing. I cannot recall a single person who has not, at some point, internalized a catastrophic incident as their own fault, as something they could have avoided. Our brains crave understanding and thrive on the illusion that we have control. When an event doesn't fit neatly into a narrative, our broken mental scripts and internalized messaging can default to self-blame. This is especially common for those raised in environments where blame was handed out indiscriminately, such as homes where alcoholism, drug addiction, and mental illness prevailed.

Healing for One Is Healing for Many

If I asked you how many people have been affected by your trauma could you give me the number? Even if it was only one more than you, is that not enough? Is it not sufficient that even one person's life was altered? A few empowering metaphors I utilize in the counseling rooms that create a visual to solidify my points on suffering are "maximize on your pain" and "cash in on your pain," and "don't waste your suffering."

To cash in and not waste what we have been through, we must identify the who's, how many, and how much. Ask yourself who has been afflicted by this experience with you, either directly or indirectly? How long have they carried part of your burden? And lastly, how did it affect their lives? As you make mental, typed, or written notes, specify how your unresolved emotional injuries influenced each individual life—not so you can spiral into guilt, shame, or disappointment in yourself, but for the sake of awareness of the power in numbers.

Unfortunately, our broken pieces are often passed on to those we love and those within our circle—so why can't the same be true for the healing in our lives? The only requirement is a willingness to accept that journey, even when it hurts, feels uncomfortable, or seems uncertain.

You did not endure the heart-wrenching events that left you confused, disoriented in life, feeling abandoned, or tempted to believe that hope for something better was unrealistic. What if you began your healing by leaning into the idea that your restoration can also create space for others to find wholeness if they choose to?

Section 3

TALK ABOUT IT!

Exercises
That Produce Real Change

6

THE EXERCISES THAT PRODUCE CHANGE

Exercise: Speak It. Write It. Heal.

To release the false burden of responsibility and recycle the truth until your mind accepts it, I invite you to complete the exercises that follow where you will speak and write a personal proclamation. You can repeat this as many times as needed, only try to keep track of how many times it has taken you to rehearse the statement until you begin to feel the neutralizing of the misaligned thoughts.

Step 1: Speak It

Take a deep breath.

Recite after me three times. You will need to hear it several times before you truly zoom into what you are saying:

I receive grace unto myself and accept that I did not deserve the various events and circumstances that occurred in my life. I did not have control over situations due to my age, state of mind, fear, and unforeseen circumstances. I choose to release responsibility and accept that it is okay to not carry accountability for what occurred. From this point forward, I choose to heal. I will agree with the truth, confront lies, and walk in peace. Where there is verified responsibility, I choose to never make the same choices again. I will make life better for myself and others from this point forward.

Step 2: Speak It Again

Recite the proclamation aloud two more times. It is most efficient when you process the proclamation line by line. Take your time and enjoy the words that can reframe your mindset.

Step 3: Write Your Pronouncement

After repeating the pronouncement above, compose your own version. You may use my version as a sample. Before you begin to write, I would encourage you to move at your own pace. Allow your mind, brain, body, and spirit to come into alignment, which in turn begins to release what has been stored up in more than one place. Once you begin this exercise, your mind and brain should find its momentum, and the processing may even begin to pour out with affirmations you never expected.

Step 4: Repetition for Internalization

Practice this exercise several times, as many times as you need, for as long as you need. Once you feel the emptying of the burden of accusation, you know something has been resolved and released.

Step 5: Journal Your Process

Now, journal about your process. Be detailed and date your journal entry. Talk about how challenging it was when you first started, identify the disconnected feelings, and reflect on what finally helped you recognize the emotional hurdles you needed to walk through during this process.

As you write about your process, your brain begins to engage with the information, recording your thoughts and feelings. This creates reinforcement, helping your brain rewire. Over time, your mind may start applying these insights to similar past experiences, hopefully leaving you wanting to do it more.

PROCESS WITH ME

I realize you are not in a consultation room, but I want you to finish strong by processing with me. This approach remains valuable, even if you complete it while alone. Begin by imagining that I am there with you. Then, share what you experienced through the *Talk About It* exercise—spoken aloud. Use as many precise, expressive words as possible.

1. What happened?

2. What did you feel?

3. What did you think?

4. What did you change your mind about?

5. What did you push out of your mind?

6. What decisions have you made regarding your past experiences as a result of this experience?

Exercise: Rewriting the Stories You Tell Yourself

The following statements are not specific to one issue. See if any of these beliefs sound familiar to you, and take an inventory to determine how often you use them. I have included a short exercise for you to complete. One effective way to heal is by thinking, writing, and speaking out loud. This is a variation of what I use to empower individuals to reframe, rewrite, and rewire their foundational beliefs. Dedicate your time to each statement. You may notice that one feels more impactful than the others. This is normal, as it shows you are responding to what is active in your mind. There is no right or wrong answer, and please refrain from judging your thoughts or labeling them as wrong, dumb, mean, etc.

Exercise: Rewire Your Thinking

1. Faultfinding Statement
   Theme: Self-Blame / Unrealistic Expectation
   Faultfinding Statement:
   I should have known better.

Confronting Question:

How could you have known what was coming, especially things you were never taught or were prepared for?

Your Turn – Rewrite & Speak

Rewrite this statement in your own words:

____

____

____

____

____

____

Say it out loud to yourself.

Exercise: Rewire Your Thinking

2. Faultfinding Statement
   Theme: Self-Blame / Misplacing Responsibility
   Faultfinding Statement:
   I brought this on myself.

Confronting Question:

What evidence is there that you caused someone else's careless or selfish choices when every person is responsible for their own behavior?

Your Turn – Rewrite & Speak

Rewrite this statement in your own words:

____

____

____

____

____

____

Say it out loud to yourself.

Exercise: Rewire Your Thinking

3. Faultfinding Statement
   Theme: Minimizing / Dismissing Feelings
   Faultfinding Statement:
   I am making this out to be much bigger than it really is.

Confronting Question:

If this wasn't a big deal, why do you still carry the effects?

Your Turn – Rewrite & Speak

Rewrite this statement in your own words:

____

____

____

____

____

____

Say it out loud to yourself.

Exercise: Rewire Your Thinking

4. Faultfinding Statement
   Theme: Shaming / Weakness Belief
   Faultfinding Statement:
   I am just weak and need to move on.

Confronting Question:

How is your need to heal not a sign of strength, being that healing requires inner power?

Your Turn – Rewrite & Speak

Rewrite this statement in your own words:

____

____

____

____

____

____

Say it out loud to yourself.

Exercise: Rewire Your Thinking

5. Faultfinding Statement
   Theme: Self Reliance/ Isolating from Help
   Faultfinding Statement:
   I should not have needed help.

Confronting Question:

Where did you learn that the best way to heal is alone? Would you expect your loved ones to carry their pain by themselves? If not, why should it be any different for you?

Your Turn – Rewrite & Speak

Rewrite this statement in your own words:

____

____

____

____

____

____

Say it out loud to yourself.

Exercise: Rewire Your Thinking

6. Faultfinding Statement
   Theme: Comparison / Minimization
   Faultfinding Statement:
   Others experienced the same thing without such emotional effects.

Confronting Question:

Two things can be true at the same time: others have experienced emotional effects, yet it is completely appropriate for you to have your own needs. Why do your necessities and your recovery have to look the same way?

Your Turn – Rewrite & Speak

Rewrite this statement in your own words:

____

____

____

____

____

____

Say it out loud to yourself.

Exercise: Rewire Your Thinking

7. Faultfinding Statement
   Theme: Rushing Healing/ Rushed Recovery
   Faultfinding Statement:
   Everyone suffers, so I need to get over it.

Confronting Question:

Whose healing timeline are you attempting to fulfill? If you listen to your inner voices, you may find that you are trying to accommodate someone else's expectations of you because they have never been comfortable facing trauma and pain, which makes life less uncomfortable for them. Maybe you even believe it's your job to never have needs.

Your Turn – Rewrite & Speak

Rewrite this statement in your own words:

____

____

____

____

____

____

Say it out loud to yourself.

Exercise: Rewire Your Thinking

8. Faultfinding Statement
   Theme: Self-Blame / Questioning Decisions
   Faultfinding Statement:
   If I knew they were going to harm me, why did I keep coming around them?

Confronting Question:

What survival instincts, attachment needs, or hopes for safety were influencing your decisions at that time—needs you did not feel you could shut off?

Your Turn – Rewrite & Speak

Rewrite this statement in your own words:

____
____
____
____
____
____

Say it out loud to yourself.

Exercise: Rewire Your Thinking

9. Faultfinding Statement
   Theme: Self-Blame / Over-Intellectualizing
   Faultfinding Statement:
   If I were smarter, I could have avoided this.

Confronting Question:

How could intelligence alone have protected you from someone else's hidden deception or manipulation?

Your Turn – Rewrite & Speak

Rewrite this statement in your own words:

____

____

____

____

____

____

Say it out loud to yourself.

Exercise: Rewire Your Thinking

10. Faultfinding Statement
    Theme: Guilt / Responsibility Misplacement
    Faultfinding Statement:
    I caused them to act this way.

Confronting Question:

What proof do you have that you controlled someone else's will, choices, or character—something no human can ever have the power to do?

Your Turn – Rewrite & Speak

Rewrite this statement in your own words:

____

____

____

____

____

____

Say it out loud to yourself.

Exercise: Rewire Your Thinking

11. Faultfinding Statement
    Theme: Self-Blame / Hindsight Distortion
    Faultfinding Statement:
    How did I not see this coming?

Confronting Question:

Is it true that you should have seen this coming, or are you judging the past with knowledge you didn't have then?

Your Turn – Rewrite & Speak

Rewrite this statement in your own words:

____

____

____

____

____

____

Say it out loud to yourself.

Exercise: Rewire Your Thinking

12. Faultfinding Statement
    Theme: Doubt / Minimization of Experience
    Faultfinding Statement:
    I may be making this up or exaggerating what happened.

Confronting Question:

The brain wants to protect you from traumatic memories. While it is possible that you do not remember every single event accurately, why does your body remember the details with such emotional truth?

Your Turn – Rewrite & Speak

Rewrite this statement in your own words:

____

____

____

____

____

____

Say it out loud to yourself.

Exercise: Rewire Your Thinking

13. Faultfinding Statement
    Theme: Self-Blame / Unrealistic Responsibility
    Faultfinding Statement:
    Why didn't I stop this?

Confronting Question:

When events occur in childhood—even into the teenage years—we often do not have the maturity, cognitive reasoning, or confidence to address matters that belong to adults. Even as adults, we may lack the inner strength or support needed to stop certain situations. Is it really true that you could have stopped what happened, considering your age, circumstances, or state of mind?

Your Turn – Rewrite & Speak

Rewrite this statement in your own words:

____

____

____

____

____

____

Say it out loud to yourself.

Exercise: Rewire Your Thinking

14. Faultfinding Statement
    Theme: Shaming / Sensitivity Belief
    Faultfinding Statement:
    I am too sensitive.

Confronting Question:

Sensitivity can be useful, and on the other side of the coin, it can reflect an exaggerated emotional response when a person has not developed a healthy framework for emotional regulation. However, sensitivity related to a past shocking event is different from sensitivity in everyday matters, such as experiencing intolerance to people's opinions or belief systems. In this context, sensitivity refers to how an individual may shame their own responses and needs connected to the lasting effects of the event. Why is feeling deeply something to be ashamed of?

Your Turn – Rewrite & Speak

Rewrite this statement in your own words:

____
____
____
____
____
____

Say it out loud to yourself.

Exercise: Rewire Your Thinking

15. Faultfinding Statement
    Theme: Comparison / Minimizing Experience
    Faultfinding Statement:
    Others have gone through worse than me.

Confronting Question:

How does someone else's suffering change the validity of yours? Isn't pain still pain?

Your Turn – Rewrite & Speak

Rewrite this statement in your own words:

____

____

____

____

____

____

Say it out loud to yourself.

Exercise: Rewire Your Thinking

16. Faultfinding Statement
    Theme: Guilt / Punishment Belief
    Faultfinding Statement:
    This is what I get for my choices.

Confronting Question:

Was it really your choices that invited this event into your life? How do your choices make someone else's wrongdoing acceptable?

Your Turn – Rewrite & Speak

Rewrite this statement in your own words:

____

____

____

____

____

____

Say it out loud to yourself.

Why These Thoughts Matter

These are just a few of the most recurring, shame-based thought patterns, more prevailing than you may realize. Narrowed down, each carries a form of unjustified remorse, shame, and embarrassment. Some may report experiencing a sick feeling that stirs in their stomach when they begin to think about the event. Some people may notice a physical slouch, emphasizing what the mouth may not be saying, while the mind is still playing out. Either way, you can be assured that if you have made any of the comments listed above, you may have found fault within yourself instead of receiving the grace and empathy you deserve as a recipe to heal.

While every life-altering experience is different, there is a series of questions that can actually be applied to most situations that have left behind the residue of trauma. It is sort of an accelerated process that can actually *disarm the trauma* by confronting the wounds with questions that will demand the truth from yourself and even from your brain. To clarify, I am not suggesting that this series of reflective questioning is the answer to every reader's issues. It is a proven tactic that has worked for people like myself, and many others who have had the most intense forms of harrowing experiences, and even those whose cases may not have been as disheartening.

In this field, I have become well-versed in the art of asking a lot of questions. This principle is something I apply to myself and those I am helping. It is a tool to dismantle false narratives and assumptions, and I invite you to adopt the regimen for yourself. You will be amazed at the lies you will uncover!

This section would not be complete without a personal decree. You might be asking what I mean by that. The words that come out of your mouth are life or burdens, truths or lies. And now that you rewrote the fault-finding statements that have been incubated and have shared aloud the reframing statements, we will close this exercise with a pronouncement that will solidify the reframing of distorted beliefs.

Exercise: Personal Decree

I am worthy of healing every broken and afflicted portion in my mind and body. I disown the fault-finding antagonist in my personal experiences that have affected me beyond my control. I am no longer responsible for carrying the weight of the events that altered my emotional, physical, and even spiritual well-being. I choose to believe that I deserve to heal without judgment, rush, or limitation.

I release self-blame, responsibility, and minimization that have resisted truth. I abandon all accusations of weakness, temptations to isolate, and the unnecessary urge to compare my own need to heal with others'. I accept the journey and the time I need to be restored. I disown the pressure of rushing, and the torment of overthinking.

I am free from the false comfort I experience by attempting to control what cannot be governed. I hand over responsibility to the appropriate weight bearers—those who willingly participated in my affliction, and those circumstances outside of my power. I decree that the truth sets me free.

The Payoff of Pain: What Clients Gain by Not Getting Better

It is hard for me to accept that people have chosen to believe that healing is not possible, even though there is evidence and opinions to the contrary. What is the payoff of choosing to stay there? Reasons may vary, but maybe there are financial benefits to maintaining the current status.

Another more common, but not often realized perspective, is the amount of attention it gains them. Some people have learned that life's detriments are the only thing that engage their loved ones with compassion, patience, and understanding. Resolving trauma releases us from the need to gain emotional connection in that manner, which only reinforces the hypervigilant, impaired, and fragmented portions of ourselves.

Years ago, I met a woman who had endless appointments for various physical ailments. Through our conversations, I began to see that many of her symptoms were psychosomatic—that is, her mind and emotional state were contributing to the physical discomfort she experienced. There were only so many days in between each doctor's appointment. In time I learned more about the embedded history that warranted her need for emotional mending, but this type of healing only begins to happen when an individual does their own searching with or without the help of another.

If you suspect this may be occurring in your life, with or without your awareness, take a moment for the following exercise. This activity will guide you through a set of questions where you can ask yourself specific points to consider.

Stay mindful, or the brain will jump in like a loaded gun to protect what has been around for quite a while. It guards the status quo. Let's go!

Exercise: Be Honest—What is This Giving You?

Not every reader will connect with this exercise, but for some, it may feel very true to their situation. For others, it may have just alerted you to something you were not expecting, and that is acceptable. Sometimes, when the diagram is laid out, it hits us: "Oh my goodness—that's me."

Exercise: Are You Holding Brokenness Patterns?

Does the illness give you what you need from people?
Answer:

Describe what it provides for you, such as comfort, peace, a sense of safety, or other feelings.
Answer:

Are there external benefits—financial, social, or other resources—that you are maintaining through this status of mental health issues?
Answer:

What might you be afraid would happen if you no longer carried this pattern or identity?
Answer:

If none of these patterns are serving you, what would be the benefits of putting your energy into your healing path?
Answer:

What part of this challenges you the most?
Answer:

Where do you feel this exercise in your body? How does it show up physically?
Answer:

What would it look like to respond differently next time?
Answer:

What support or resources could help you on this path?
Answer:

What is the most important thing you've learned about yourself through these reflections?
Answer:

Trauma as a Trend

I am aware that trauma has been abused as a trend and aggressively pushed through the social media world to our younger generations. They are being guided to disconnect from people who truly love them. Trauma has been used as permission to stay unhealed, unforgiving, and hopeless. The hopelessness is because many, not just the younger generations, have been told that the answer to their healing is completely doing away with those who have wounded them.

Trust me when I say that as a therapist, coach, faith counselor and leader, I have visited hundreds upon hundreds of cases with some of the most excruciating, inhumane details.

Sitting with clients day after day, even up to 10 hours a day at times, I can assure you that you begin to understand some of the people that harmed them were also victims of a shattered or traumatic upbringing themselves. Of course, there are the occasional individuals who made a decision long ago that they would live life as wickedly as possible, but these are the few exceptions.

There are some contexts that put a demand on the question, "Did your (parents, wife, husband, etc.) have a rough upbringing?" When I ask this, immediately the client begins to narrate the often horrific details of their loved one's history—the very one that contributed to the broken pieces of my client's life. They quickly *disconnect* themselves from the person, and for a brief moment, see them through the lens of an observer and even a therapist.

What if you are the person being spoken about in a therapy session? Have you considered the possibility that someone holds injuries against you? I know I have scattered many of the damaged pieces of me onto my own children and other family members. The healed version of me wishes I could take it all back and deposit healthy instead.

I have learned through professional and personal experience that as long as you have not yet mended, yet alone identified what needs restoring within you, it will be harder to accept that you, I, and all of us well-meaning beings can duplicate our psychological injuries in different ways.

As people, our initial response is often to reject the possibility that we may have been wrong in the first place, even when our reasoning is well trained. This is a double-edged reality. The first edge lies in our minds, which is part of the life force of who you are. When this part of you and me is matured in truth, character, and the internal, all-consuming decision to walk in a manner that is loving, kind, responsible, thoughtful, and intentional, it becomes easier to take responsibility for incoming information—even that which holds us accountable. It can bypass the brain's natural resistance.

When the response is denial, the result is accumulated resentment, frustration, disappointment, and maybe even being cut off from family, spouses, and other important relationships. Please note that I do not generally endorse the family cut-off method that is overtaking our American culture and keeping members of our society from being mature in healthy confrontation and boundaries. Unless there is physical or sexual abuse, I believe most issues can be worked out, even if you have to assert some heavy-hitting boundaries. Remember, this is what I do for hours in a day at the time of the writing of this book.

The human tendency is to justify and push away the possibility that we broke someone from the inside out. I have been there. You have been there. We have all been there. Recall the information I have relayed throughout the book. The brain's job is to protect us. When someone shares a grievance, we immediately go into self-justification and protection mode. This summons the psychological defense, which can look like purposeful denial. Denial is not always a deliberate rejection of reality; it can actually be a protective response which needs to be discussed and unraveled.

Facing the Damage You Left Behind

I believe most of humanity carries some level of trauma. And those who don't were likely raised in an idealized version of family life that most of us only used to see portrayed on television long ago. What is very clear to me is that every person who comes in to see me with trauma may have also contributed to trauma in someone else's life.

Pause for a moment. I don't want my statement to gut-punch you or throw you into a maelstrom of emotion, leaving you frantically wondering who you have wounded. To understand how this could possibly be, it is beneficial to understand that trauma can also be defined by each person's individual experience. It is typically understood in two parts: first, by the way they interpreted the event; and second, by the psychological impact it has had on that person.

What one person interprets through their emotional, physical, and spiritual state is determined by how they internalize the event. And internationalization is dependent upon various factors such as previous experiences and traumas, upbringing and environment, and even their belief systems. No two people will typically receive an event in the exact same manner.

Having laid out a foundation for understanding an individual's trauma response, I want to get into the thick of it and say that even when we begin to look at the details of how someone may perceive and be affected by an event, it does not mean that we are always empathetic to the pain we have caused someone. As a parent, partner, and leader in multiple domains, I can assure you that I have met many individuals who deflected, minimized, or rationalized their past behaviors. And if we are honest, even you and I have been responsible for such behaviors and responses at some point in someone's conversation and valid claims.

No one likes to look at themselves and say, "Wow, I was messed up." Or, at least most of us don't. But it is possible to have had such an impact on a person.

Making Your Apology Count

What is the best way to navigate these events? Ready for it? First, we will have to get used to admitting the things most of us do not take pleasure in—knowing we wounded someone we care for and love. Second, we will need to come to grips with the specific ways in which we did cause injury. This part looks different, and the only person that has the information on the effects is the person that incurred them. Lastly, it is taking responsibility and apologizing in a repentant and specific manner. That means that an apology—and possibly several of them at various times in life—will look and sound pointed at your errors.

An intentional apology will never sound off with, "I am sorry *if* I hurt you." We know when we afflicted someone because it was either intentional or they told you about it. Of course, there are the ones that never told you, but charged you mightily along the way with passive-aggressive accusations and behaviors, which I will address in a bit. But the bulk of hurts can be resolved by a thorough conversation—a hard one, nonetheless.

A productive conversation can look something like this:

"Son, I have been thinking about the many years where I was gone from your life. I realize that I took so much from you by not being there. I know that had to be harder than I will ever know. I know you missed out on a dad being there while your friends all had theirs to support them. You must have felt all alone. I wish I could take back time and make it better, and I realize that nothing will give you back those days and years. I am working on healing, and I intend to make it better, so please feel free to let me know how exactly I can be there for you. Please know, I will not be perfect, but don't let that discourage you from speaking up. I have people in my inner circle holding me accountable and guiding me in this journey. The one who truly knows what you need through this is you. I love you and hope you will forgive me for my selfishness. If there is anything you would like to know, feel free to ask so I can help you heal as well. And I also accept that your healing may take time and be done in portions. I am willing to give you time and support as you do."

Their Healing May Take Time, Be Patient

The one thing you will have to understand is that this may be a powerful contribution to the strayed relationship, but it does not guarantee healing for them, especially not immediately. It also does not mean the person receiving your apology will accept it. An illusion that follows this activity is that all will be well instantly. This may be true for some, but not for all. Individuals have to process the many years the injuries existed, plus the seasons they spent cultivating the injuries in their heart, and brain. We never know what life has looked like for those we wounded, so the process is unpredictable.

You are only responsible for yourself—your reactions and your responses to their resistance. Make it a point to wait well.

When Unforgiveness is Their Choice

The ones who suffer with unforgiveness have made up their mind that no sort of confession of faults will fix your transgressions. This could be a temporary but long-term reaction as they may not have been prepared for that moment. Others may go as far as declaring that they would rather die than give you their pardon. In choosing offense over healing, they are holding their own restoration hostage.

Those in my counseling spaces will hear that we must allow people the space to choose. In time, you can try again. If it doesn't work the second time, allow some space and see what unfolds.

In the end, as one of my church family members says, "You have to let them do the work. You have done yours." It doesn't mean to flagrantly dismiss them and become offended because they won't choose to heal and accept this moment. In fact, the apology may very well be the first step only. Be patient. Many of them have been hurting for years, therefore it may take some time for them to reflect on your words.

I know that for many of you, your apology may have been conceived from the purest, deepest, most regretful places of your heart. You may have come to a once blinded realization of the power of your actions, and how they have damaged others, some for many years now. You may have taken time for deep thoughts, reflections, and even prayers. But even then, the recipient may, in the end, accuse you of making excuses for sharing the background of events going on in your life during those periods.

It is possible that more than one thing can be true at the same time. You can hold a remorseful stance, and attempt to speak of where your mindset was in life.

What I have learned is that everyone is different. Some individuals who have been impacted want to understand the "why" behind your transgressions, while others find it insulting—a form of denying your responsibility.

You may cry, grieve, and regret again and again. And you may even have to choose to let them do the work several times over, as long as you have brought them your most heartfelt, excuse-free apology and have not denied their pain.

Even When it Feels Unfair: Apologizing for the Wounds Passed Down

If your apology has been tied to explanations but mistaken for excuses, and if your expression of remorse has been direct and intentional toward the pain, then you are free to breathe.

I know from experience that some of your errors may actually be the result of inheriting the mistakes of your forefathers and foremothers. You, too, were affected by someone else's mess, and perhaps you passed parts of it down yourself—but now you may be the one who has to take ownership.

This is done through your own acknowledgment and apologies for both their injuries and yours. Sadly, we all get left with someone else's crap—pardon my expression—but often, only one person ends up responsible for cleaning it up.

While it is hurtful, it is worth it. After all, is it not time to change for future generations?

Yes, it feels deeply unfair and painful to think that you contributed to someone's dysfunction because someone else broke you. There is no one to say, "Hey you! I'm sorry those things happened to you. I'm sorry that your past experiences shaped you into the least healthy version of yourself."

I understand, personally, how challenging this is. I realize that when you are the one endowed with the gift of fixing generationally broken things you also have to navigate the waves of the past in your own life, with no one else taking responsibility. But healing can happen here too. It may not feel like it at the time, but to help you get started, I have included an exercise for you.

This guided practice is meant to be processed in an intensely personal way. It will engage your soul, body, and spirit, collaborating through words that should be spoken out loud, with your name used at the proper moments. Before you begin, take a breath. This prepares your brain and whole being to receive and process the information ahead. If you feel a bodily or emotional response in any particular part of the exercise, that is most likely the place that needs to be loved, worked through, and repaired. Don't become tempted to overlook it or rush through it. Remember that breathing will be key in every prompt throughout the rest of this book. It helps calm your nervous system and reminds your brain that you are safe, and that this is a good thing!

Exercise: You Needed Healing Too

Instructions:

Repeat this out loud as many times as needed:

I (state your name) acknowledge that I have committed errors. I choose to take responsibility for all of my ways, for the pain I caused others, and for those wounds I carry from my own past and present. I accept that I, too, have been broken by the actions others have bestowed upon my life. I was broken and wired to break others, causing me to take on an identity that was never mine to begin with.

I give myself grace. This looks like understanding the history of my making—the words spoken over me, the interactions I experienced with my loved ones, and the silence meant to erase who I truly am. It was intended to warp my greatest attributes.

I will never tolerate abuse again, not from myself or from others. Those behaviors produce toxicity all around me and have long-lasting effects. Therefore, I dismiss their presence in my life.

I release myself from the guilt and condemnation for wounding others and, in the process, damaging myself by destroying the healthy family, friends, and loved ones in my life. I declare healing over their soul, over all of their being, especially their heart and mind.

I choose to speak kindly to myself to begin the healing journey. I (state your name) am truly sorry for the loving words that were never spoken over you. I apologize that you had to walk through cold and lonely days. I mourn the doubts and insecurity that were birthed through your experiences. I am deeply sorry that peace was lacking and confusion always reigned. You truly were meant for tranquility, to handle situations with poise, humility, and understanding. Anger was never supposed to be your portion; it was the result of fear.

Closing Declaration:

I receive the power of forgiveness over myself for the many places that lack empathy and comfort. I will heal and bring others with me as I continue in this journey of self-reflection, responsibility, and compassion.

Signature

____

Date

____

7

FINALLY, IT'S TIME TO TALK ABOUT IT!

So far I presented you with a background of how I operate and walk others through their restoration. I shared methods and metaphors, presented useful exercises, and now I believe you may be ready to *talk about it.*

The sequence was not accidental. As you read through the pages in order, I was attempting to disarm any potential resistance within you by providing a lighthearted way to look at all the pieces at work protecting trauma. Walking through the various steps and principles begins to alert the brain that this is safe, and it may even create a slight anticipation for the journey.

From this point forward, you are going to get real, write, speak things out loud, and even record yourself if you choose to. Before you begin your own process, I want to share an example of what it looks like to *talk about it* so that you can engage in healing principles waiting to be activated by you, and for you. This case story provided is fictional, but the issues portrayed are based on real experiences. For confidentiality and ethical purposes, nothing in here is relating to one single individual. I may even throw in some details from my own life to help you normalize healing. Before I share the account, there are a few key points that will help you ease into the stage.

Readiness is an Illusion: You Can Only Prepare

Before we begin, I gently remind you that traumatic events leave behind difficult emotional, physical, psychological, and spiritual effects. This leads me to suggest that the details disclosed below may be uneasy to take in, but they are necessary for the sake of doing the exercise effectively. It is possible that you begin the exercise, have to put it down for a bit—at times even days—then get back on it. That is totally acceptable. For some, I would not even put it past you to leave it for a couple of years.

While I want you to "be ready" to discuss your traumatic events, can I share with you that readiness is mostly an illusion? We prepare to enter into that session of processing, but readiness is not real.

To prepare, we must first give ourselves permission to enter into a discomforting state that can offer benefits. In counseling, we would call this reframing your expectations. If you view the encounter as threatening, then you will resist it. Can I invite you to take a breath and give yourself permission to unload weight that has been traveling with you from moment to moment, encounter to encounter, relationship to relationship, and much more?

Schedule Your Time for Healing

In addition to preparation, you must schedule your time with your healing. When I began writing this book, I was not sure how many chapters it would be. Initially, I assumed that I would write it based on the traditional word count that publishers push for in most non-fiction cases. Yet the more I thought about it, and the more I sought counsel from individuals who understood the writing and healing world, we came to the conclusion that writing only what I needed to say was the priority.

Secondly, producing an uncomplicated volume would be best for trauma readers anyway. I mention this to help you understand that this book was written in a succinct, straightforward manner to increase the chances of you and others with similar backgrounds to commit to reading and completing the exercises successfully.

Sacred Space

If this book and its activities become an option, so will your recovery. If you have to leave the house and go sit at a park, a grocery store parking lot, or some private place in the home to allow you personal space to unpack, that is the best space. Don't forget to consider your phone as a potential knock on the door, and you are the only one who can answer it. Silence it, or make an iron-will determination that you will not allow it to disrupt the moment.

I can assure you that in today's society, private matters—including therapy sessions and personal healing conversations—have been reduced to conversations in living rooms, no matter who else is present. Individuals have reduced these interactions to a casual, errand-driven level of priority. Others may even sit in spaces with children nearby during what should be a very important block of time.

I cannot demand that people honor their appointment as sacred, but I am speaking to you, my reader. I want you to get the best of these moments. So schedule your reading and exercise time like a very valuable and personal moment. And of course, don't forget to be fully loaded with your journal, pen, and tissues.

Forgiveness is the New "F" Word: Letting Go to Change Your Brain

Forgiveness is the new "F" word. And this section was not written to convince you to forgive someone, but to help you understand that some traumatic events held within our minds and hearts are clutched behind the unwillingness to forgive. If you look around on social media, you will find many in the healing professions who are responsible for mediating permanent disconnection within family lines, even the breaking of parental ties. Instead of coaching their clients in the area of boundaries and providing assertion training, these practitioners have inserted themselves into family ties and have shamelessly encouraged a breaking of something that could be restored with time and under the proper setup, thus eliminating the option of forgiveness altogether.

Many of you have been a victim of this trend. Some of you have chosen this on your own. Please know that I understand why someone may choose to disconnect. Space can be helpful. But scores of individuals taking this step are not looking for space;

they are looking to permanently dissolve a human being in their life that may need healing, just like them. Some may even do this to avoid confrontation, which feels very threatening to their nervous system. But that is an additional topic that proves my point as to why I chose to keep all the scientific and psychological loops out of this, so that you, as my reader, would stay engaged and enjoy a basic read. But do trust me when I tell you that the decision to remain in a state of unforgiveness really will affect your ability to process trauma and even to heal physically.

I don't believe we have to subject ourselves to physical or sexual abuse, and those are exceptions. The rest are boundaries we can set with discussions. If others choose not to engage in that manner, we are no longer responsible.

There seems to often be confusion that forgiveness equals full access or full forbearance of devastating patterns. Even then, most issues are much more complex than I could possibly write about and justify in one sitting. Every single person that I have guided who cut a very close family member off has had varying circumstances. A good bunch were salvageable with the right steps.

Explaining the previously mentioned ideas works to prepare you to go ahead and deal with the resistance that will appear within milliseconds should this apply to you.

Remember, one of the brain's most important jobs is to protect you. It does not stop to look for the facts before it decides which way to go. If you have a resistance about someone or something, so shall your brain proceed.

For that reason, I share a snippet of this information so that as you step into the "Talk About It" exercise, you take into account any potential pushback from the beginning. And if this does not apply to you, consider it useful information to share with those you know.

If you can identify with this reaction and would like to tear down the defenses, it is a very simple process to begin. It kicks off with a decision. It really is that simple. The mind decides, and the brain follows. Even if you have to practice deciding a few times, it is okay. It is a simple process considering how many years you may have been retelling yourself the hurtful stories that were reinforcing your beliefs and feelings.

Once you decide, you can begin to journey through your past events as you talk about it. If you find that even after "deciding" you are still struggling with the idea of forgiveness, then process the details of the story and the pain and shock behind it, and then you can come back to this step. This step is not always necessary as a first stop, but not mentioning it would be a disservice to anyone who desires to experience freedom.

Pick It. Stick With It.

Would you like to hear a confession? One of a therapist's or healing practitioner's least favorite clients to work with are the ones who want to make an appointment with you, but already have their diagnosis on hand. They discovered it through their favorite platform, which provided plenty of evidence for their symptoms and behaviors.

This trend has made way for a plethora of healing options, techniques, methods, theories, and spiritual approaches. I say, choose the one you feel most comfortable with and deploy it. In other words, if you find yourself critiquing or dissecting the process this book provides because you heard or saw something different through another vehicle, then regroup and use what you trust.

This way forward is meant to be simple and, hopefully, accelerated—as seen in hundreds of clients that come into my spaces—and for those who desire a focused approach they can pick and stick with.

Example of Walking Through the Words: Carla's Story

Caution: Before reading this story, please note that it contains material that may be emotionally impactful for some readers. I have avoided graphic detail, but please proceed with care.

I was only seven when life started feeling shaky. My mom had left my stepdad, who had been abusive, but leaving didn't make everything safe. He was an alcoholic, and if he became angry, he would begin to yell and scream, and things would begin to fly across the room. My siblings would run to the bedroom, and I would try to distract them or turn up the TV so they would not have to hear the arguing and fighting going on in the other room. Most of the time the storm would stop, and we would eventually go to bed, but I was always nervous that something would break out at any moment.

My mom had to work long hours to keep us afloat, and suddenly I was helping raise my younger siblings. I cooked meals, helped with homework, and tried to hold them close when the nights felt unsafe. I don't remember my mom ever telling us that everything would be okay. We were left wondering when the next moment of hell would come through.

During those days, I had endured physical and sexual abuse by several people, and that still comes back in flashes when I least expect them. Some days are worse than others, though.

One day, I was sent home from school because I was sick. When my stepdad got home, he was very angry and accused me of making it up to get to hang out at home. He made me get up from the bed after being sick, throwing up half the day, and I had to clean the house, including scrubbing the restrooms with bleach. I was sick for several days after that, but I had to fake being well to avoid severe punishment.

Nightmares are common and have been. I often wake up crying from some of the dreams. They have a recurring theme, and they feel so real. I have anger and anxiety several times a week. I get agitated easily. If I get around a lot of people, I begin to feel like I am shaking on the inside, like trembling. During times like that, anger surfaces. If I see a man with a flannel shirt, I get triggered. My stepdad wore those for work. When he walked in, his clothing stood out for some reason.

Since my mom was always stressed, she did a lot of yelling too. I was never sure when I would get in trouble for not having the house fully put together the way she demanded. Maybe she was trying to avoid the fights with my stepdad. Today, my home is a mess. I don't want to clean much. I get overwhelmed at the idea of cleaning it, but there is something comforting about not having it perfect.

Also, I decided not to have children. I am tired of looking out for others. It's just me and my dog Cody. I have been through at least three practitioners, but it has not really helped. They usually just ask me questions about my symptoms, then tell me to count, breathe, put a cold pack on my neck, take walks, etc., but it just does not solve the issues. I just want to feel better.

Disarming The Trauma: Step by Step

Below is an example of the strategies I utilize to disarm trauma and dismantle what they are carrying. These are not always exact in every case, but very close. Please do not read over these at a rapid pace. I encourage you to process them, because you will be applying these as well.

I apologize to the person for the pain they have endured:

"I am so sorry you went through this. I know I had nothing to do with what happened, but you deserve acknowledgement that this was obviously very painful, and you did not deserve that."

Acknowledge their environment:

When you grow up in an alcoholic, violent, or drug-dependent environment, the norm is usually chaos, anger, and outbursts. This leaves your nervous system shot, and your brain on alert that you are probably always in danger. You may be holding the fears of your young years. You never feel fully safe, so your system kicks up anxiety to remind you that there are unresolved issues, and you are not sure you are safe yet.

Assure their safety:

"You are safe, you are in control, and nobody can harm you." These words are powerful to a person who is frozen in the experiences they were exposed to when they were small. I ask them one question at a time: Are you safe? Are you in control? Can anyone hurt you again? They are typically able to process these, regarding the years-ago experiences, with the truths of today. Then I prescribe the proclamation of these as rewiring statements: I am safe. I am in control. Nobody can harm me."

These statements are powerful and can be repeated as many times as necessary for any event they feel would be applicable. When the pain and processing is fresh, these statements begin to disarm the pain, the trauma, and provide relief.

Even if I do not have your story, or the story of many suffering with internal chaos, I know that speaking, writing, and even recording their story for themselves on video or audio provides an outlet for the mind, brain, and body, including the nervous system, to release the intensity of the memories locked in. The steps are short and simple, but historically very effective.

Keep in mind that you may be wondering where the rest of the steps went, but I have been teaching them along the way. Even simple exercises such as "Process with Me" and "The Bully in Your Brain" are steps to transformation. You can apply these very methods and metaphors to your stories as well. Remember, that simply talking about it begins the work!

Her Story Ends, Your Story Begins

Carla's story does not have wrong details. She shared the past, specific details, and even a very strong memory of a particular event. I encourage you to do the same.

Instructions:

Write your story in detail. Do not judge the details or try to censor them. Include a story that is strongly lingering in your heart—something that feels unresolved or impactful.

Use the steps outlined earlier as you write: acknowledge the pain, assess the environment, assure safety, and practice the rewiring statements: "I am safe. I am in control. Nobody can harm me."

This approach can be applied to almost any issue, including

- A car accident
- Abuse (physical, emotional, sexual)
- Neglect or abandonment
- Family dysfunction or chaos
- Loss or grief
- Bullying or harassment
- Any experience that left you feeling unsafe, anxious, or frozen

Writing or recording your story using these steps provides an outlet for your mind, body, and nervous system, allowing the intensity of memories to begin releasing. You can repeat this process for as many stories as possible. Keep in mind that once you work through this once, the brain knows to apply the methods and techniques to future memories that need to be processed, and even future experiences.

8

CHANGE YOUR MIND: FINDING THE BETTER VERSION OF YOU

A lovely walk inspired the title of this work. Yet the truth is, it was the abundance of experiences I faced daily with numerous individuals that helped me understand the importance of something so simple, yet profound and effective for countless seekers.

I was willing to take a risk of being criticized by some in the mental health field for the simplification of this topic, and by those in the faith community for providing a supplement as a restorative tool. It has been a pleasure working through this book with both sides of the spectrum in mind. One can argue with opinion, but not my experience. As I began to write this last portion, I was reflecting on how I should end this book. I considered various directions, but I like to keep things real, so it demanded an impactful closing. I thought about my day and who I got to counsel with. Then it came to my mind that yesterday I sat with a someone who has probably seen one of the most drastic healings in my many years of working with individuals. If you only knew the details. They were dark. Lifeless. Threatening. Harmful. And many would have labeled this case as only manageable, but not redeemable or repairable.

We witnessed the opposite in their life, and now the real excitement began in the celebration of what is ahead—hope. We found ourselves unpacking future dreams for them, such as traveling worldwide, poetry and music writing, and career opportunities. Many healing professionals and everyday people would not have taken the risk to believe that this person had great potential to encounter wholeness. They might have aligned with the comfortable, risk-free side of prescribing techniques only.

Today, another person reminded me that they felt hopeful after our meeting. Thankfully, the feeling was not the only thing they acquired; it was positive outcomes as well. This was the confirmation I needed that this chapter was coming along in the direction necessary. It is daily that I hear personal accounts from individuals who state they were not given the option to attempt to heal. I don't say this in a critical manner, but in the fullness of exhortation—change your mind! If you are the one seeking relief from the past, adopt the belief that you are not required to stay the same. The choice is up to you.

Change your mind because the better version of you is on the other side of cynicism. Simplify the ideas that challenge your hope so that you can get to the trauma that your past left behind.

Don't look for permission and affirmation from others. You don't require a family member's diagnosis of your memory's torments. You lived them! That is all the proof you need. Remember to heal to be whole, not to discard blame and accusation, as that is not attaining healing; it is simply transferring the results of your pain onto them.

When we are intentional, the movement begins.

HAPPY HEALING!!

Glossary

The Healing Framework

The concepts in this glossary are organized within a simple healing framework developed through years of working with individuals navigating trauma, emotional pain, and internal conflict. The goal is not theory—it is transformation.

Breakthrough:

Experiencing something one never thought would be possible.

Bully in Your Brain:

A symbolic construct that appears as a shadowy tornado with a grumpy face that sits right before your brain to threaten, shout out thoughts, imagination, and limit what comes in and what goes out.

Disarming the Trauma:

Facing a memory and releasing the lies, judgments, and feelings it holds—those that keep you trapped in the power of that event in your mind.

Dormant Active Grief:

Active grief that remains through unresolved trauma and lies in the shadows, quietly influencing thoughts, emotions, and behaviors, often causing unexplained or unrecognized symptoms. It is the kind of grief sufferers may not even realize is affecting them.

Grief:

Grief is the profound emotional and total soul reaction to the loss of something, not just someone.

Impurities:
Any attached unhealthy meaning to my suffering.

Mental Metaphors:
Mental metaphors make abstract concepts concrete, creating a pathway for insight, coping, and healing.

Process with Me:
The invitation for clients to engage in a powerful way with what has been said, debunked, challenged, established, interpreted, redefined, analyzed, and any other phenomena that occurred within those short minutes.

Soul:
An invisible part of the human being known as the inner person that hosts the mind, will, emotions, and intellect.

The Soul Demands Healing:
When your life force demands that its tormented portions express itself through untamable outbursts, eruptions, or even more gentle seeping.

Talk About It:
Sharing past trauma, either by speaking with another person, writing about it, or verbalizing it to oneself, as a means of processing and healing.

Triggers:
Powerful signals of unhealed patterns, experiences, and beliefs that lead you into healing.

Change Your Mind:
The intentional shift in perspective, belief, and interpretation that allows transformation and healing.

Rewiring Statements:
Simple, present-tense declarations used to reinforce safety and truth in the nervous system, e.g., "I am safe. I am in control. Nobody can harm me."

Disclaimer

The information in Talk About It! Healing the Trauma Your Past Left Behind reflects the author's accumulated wisdom and insights from years of providing guidance to individuals seeking personal growth, healing, and self-understanding. It is provided for educational and informational purposes only and is not intended to diagnose, treat, or prevent any mental, emotional, or physical health condition, nor should it be considered a substitute for professional counseling, psychotherapy, or medical care.

Reading this book does not create a counselor–client relationship between the reader and the author. The content is offered for general insight, reflection, and personal development. Readers are encouraged to seek qualified professional support when needed. Neither the author nor the publisher assumes liability for any loss, damage, or adverse outcome resulting from the application of information contained in this book.

Call or text 988 for the Suicide and Crisis Lifeline for immediate assistance.

www.ingramcontent.com/pod-product-compliance
Lightning Source LLC
LaVergne TN
LVHW022053200926
848481LV00003B/888
9798234111616